Novels for Students, Volume 2

Copyright © 1997

Gale Research
835 Penobscot Building
645 Griswold St.
Detroit, Ml 48226-4094

ISBN 0-7876-1687-7
ISSN 1094-3552

Printed in the United States of America
10 9 8 7 6 5 4

The House on Mango Street

Sandra Cisneros

1983

Introduction

The House on Mango Street, which appeared in 1983, is a linked collection of forty-four short tales that evoke the circumstances and conditions of a Hispanic American ghetto in Chicago. The narrative is seen through the eyes of Esperanza Cordero, an adolescent girl coming of age. These concise and poetic tales also offer snapshots of the roles of women in this society. They uncover the dual forces that pull Esperanza to stay rooted in her cultural traditions on the one hand, and those that compel her to pursue a better way of life outside the *barrio* on the other. Throughout the book Sandra Cisneros explores themes of cultural tradition, gender roles, and coming of age in a binary society that struggles to hang onto its collective past while integrating itself into the American cultural landscape. Cisneros wrote the vignettes while struggling with her identity as an author at the University of Iowa's Writers Workshop in the 1970s. She was influenced by Russian-born novelist and poet Vladimir Nabokov's memoirs and by her own experiences as a child in the Chicago *barrio*. This engaging book has brought the author critical acclaim and a 1985 Before Columbus American Book Award. Specifically, it has been highly lauded for its impressionistic, poetic style and powerful imagery. Though Cisneros is a young writer and her work is not plentiful, *The House on Mango Street* establishes her as a major figure in American literature. Her work has already been the subject of numerous scholarly studies and is often at the forefront of works that explore the role of Latinas in American society.

Author Biography

The experiences of Esperanza, the adolescent protagonist of *The House on Mango Street*, closely resemble those of Sandra Cisneros's childhood. The author was born to a Mexican father and a Mexican American mother in 1954 in Chicago, Illinois, the only daughter of seven children. The family, for whom money was always in short supply, frequently moved between the ghetto neighborhoods of Chicago and the areas of Mexico where her father's family lived. Cisneros remembers that as a child she often felt a sense of displacement. By 1966 her parents had saved enough money for a down payment on a rundown, two-story house in a decrepit Puerto Rican neighborhood on Chicago's north side. There Cisneros spent much of her childhood. This house, as well as the colorful group of characters Cisneros observed around her in the *barrio*, served as inspiration for some of the stories in *The House on Mango Street*.

The author once remarked, "Because we moved so much, and always in neighborhoods that appeared like France after World War II—empty lots and burned-out buildings—I retreated inside myself." Cisneros was an introspective child with few friends; her mother encouraged her to read and write at a young age, and made sure her daughter had her own library card. The author wrote poems and stories as a schoolgirl, but the impetus for her career as a creative writer came during her college years, when she was introduced to the works of Donald Justice, James Wright, and other writers who made Cisneros more aware of her cultural roots.

Cisneros graduated from Loyola University in 1976 with a B.A. in English. She began to pursue graduate studies in writing at the University of Iowa, and earned a Master of Fine Arts degree in creative writing in 1978. Cisneros says that through high school and college, she did not perceive herself as being different from her fellow English majors. She spoke Spanish only at home with her father, but otherwise wrote and studied within the mainstream of American literature. At the University of Iowa Writers' Workshop, Cisneros found her true voice as an author. Compared with her more privileged, wealthier classmates from more stable environments, Cisneros's cultural difference as a Chicana became clear. Though at first she imitated the style and tone of acclaimed American authors, Cisneros came to realize that her experience as a Hispanic woman differed from that of her classmates and offered an opportunity to develop her own voice. Cisneros once remarked, "Everyone seemed to have some communal knowledge which I did not have—My classmates were from the best schools in the country. They had been bred as fine hothouse flowers. I was a yellow weed among the city's cracks." The author began to explore her past experiences, which served as the inspiration of many of her stories and distinguished her from her peers. Her master's thesis, *My Wicked Wicked Ways* (Iowa, 1978, published as a book in 1987) is a collection of poems that begins to explore daily experiences, encounters, and observations in this new-found voice.

Cisneros has held several fellowships that have allowed her to focus on her writing full-time. These awards have enabled her to travel to Europe and to other parts of the United States, including a stint in Austin, Texas, where she experienced another thriving community of Latin American culture. She has also taught creative writing and worked with students at the Latino Youth Alternative High School in Chicago.

The House on Mango Street is the coming of age story of Esperanza Cordero, a preadolescent Mexican American girl (Chicana) living in the contemporary United States. A marked departure from the traditional novel form, *The House on Mango Street* is a slim book consisting of forty-four vignettes, or literary sketches, narrated by Esperanza and ranging in length from two paragraphs to four pages. In deceptively simple language, the novel recounts the complex experience of being young, poor, female, and Chicana in America. The novel opens with a description of the Cordero family's house on Mango Street, the most recent in a long line of houses they have occupied. Esperanza is dissatisfied with the house, which is small and cramped, and doesn't want to stay there. But Mango Street is her home now, and she sets out to try to understand it.

Mango Street is populated by people with many different life stories, stories of hope and despair. First there is Esperanza's own family: her kind father who works two jobs and is absent most of the time; her mother, who can speak two languages and sing opera but never finished high school; her two brothers Carlos and Kiki; and her little sister Nenny. Of the neighborhood children Esperanza meets, there is Cathy, who shows her around Mango Street but moves out shortly thereafter because the neighborhood is "getting bad." Then there are Rachel and Lucy, sisters from Texas, who become Esperanza and Nenny's best friends. There is Meme, who has a dog with two names, one in Spanish and one in English, and Louie the boy from Puerto Rico whose cousin steals a Cadillac one day and gives all the children a ride.

Then there are the teenage girls of Mango Street, whom Esperanza studies carefully for clues about becoming a woman. There is Marin from Puerto Rico, who sells Avon cosmetics and takes care of her younger cousins, but is waiting for a boyfriend to change her life. There is Alicia, who must take care of her father and siblings because her mother is dead, but is determined to keep going to college. And there is Esperanza's beautiful friend Sally, who marries in the eighth grade in order to get away from her father but is now forbidden by her husband to see her friends. Esperanza, Nenny, Lucy, and Rachel discover that acting sexy is more dangerous than liberating when a neighbor gives them four pairs of hand-me-down high heels. They strut around the neighborhood acting like the older girls until a homeless man accosts them. After fleeing, the girls quickly take off the shoes with the intention of never wearing them again.

The grown women Esperanza comes across on Mango Street are less daring and hopeful than the teenage girls, but they have acquired the wisdom that comes with experience. They advise Esperanza not to give up her independence in order to become a girlfriend or wife. Her Aunt Lupe, who was once pretty and strong but is now dying, encourages

Esperanza to write poetry. Her mother, who was once a good student, a "smart cookie," regrets having dropped out of school. There are other women in the neighborhood who don't fit into either category, like Edna's Ruthie, a grownup who "likes to play." While the text implies that Ruthie is developmentally disabled, Esperanza perceives her as somebody who "sees lovely things everywhere."

Through observing and interacting with her neighbors, Esperanza forms a connection to Mango Street which conflicts with her desire to leave. At the funeral for Rachel and Lucy's baby sister she meets their three old aunts who read her palm and her mind:

> Esperanza. The one with marble hands called me aside. Esperanza. She held my face with her blueveined hands and looked and looked at me. A long silence. When you leave you must remember always to come back, she said.
>
> What?
>
> When you leave you must remember to come back for the others. A circle, understand? You will always be Esperanza. You will always be Mango Street. You can't erase what you know. You can't forget who you are.
>
> Then I didn't know what to say. It was as if she could read my mind, as

if she knew what I had wished for,
and I felt ashamed for having made
such a selfish wish.

You must remember to come back.
For the ones who cannot leave as
easily as you. You will remember?
She asked as if she was telling me.
Yes, yes, I said a little confused.

The three sisters tell Esperanza that while she
will go far in life she must remember to come back
to Mango Street for the others who do not get as far.
By the novel's end Esperanza has realized that her
writing is one way to maintain the connection to
Mango Street without having to give up her own
independence. She will tell the stories of the "ones
who cannot out."

Characters

Alicia

"Alicia Who Sees Mice" is a young woman burdened by taking care of her family while attending college in order to escape her way of life in the *barrio*. She is only afraid of mice, which serve as a metaphor for her poverty.

Cathy

Cathy, "Queen of Cats," as Esperanza calls her because of her motley collection of felines, is one of Esperanza's neighborhood playmates. Cathy tells Esperanza that she and her family are leaving because the neighborhood into which Esperanza has just moved is going downhill.

Carlos Cordero

Carlos is Esperanza's younger brother. The brothers have little interaction with Esperanza and Nenny outside of the structure of the household.

Esperanza Cordero

"In English my name means hope. In Spanish it means too many letters," says Esperanza Cordero. In a childlike voice, Esperanza records impressions of the world around her. Her perceptions range from humorous anecdotes pulled from life in the *barrio* to more dark references to crime and sexual provocation. Through Esperanza's eyes, the reader catches short yet vivid glimpses of the other characters, particularly the females in Esperanza's neighborhood. In part, Esperanza finds her sense of selfidentity among these women. With a sense of awe and mystery, for example, she looks to older girls who wear black clothes and makeup. She experiments with womanhood herself in "The Family of Little Feet," a story in which Esperanza and her friends cavort about the neighborhood in high heel shoes, but are forced to flee when they attract unwanted male attention. Esperanza's sense of selfidentity is also interwoven with her family's house, which emerges throughout the book as an important metaphor for her circumstances. She longs for her own house, which serves as a symbol of the stability, financial means, and sense of belonging that she lacks in her environment: "a house all my own—Only a house quiet as snow, a space for myself to go, clean as paper before the poem."

As the stories develop, Esperanza matures. She turns from looking outward at her world to a more introspective viewpoint that reveals several sides of her character. Esperanza is a courageous girl who recognizes the existence of a bigger world beyond her constraining neighborhood, and who, toward the end of the book, is compelled by her own inner strength to leave the *barrio*. Nonetheless, Esperanza demonstrates empathy for those around her, particularly those who do not see beyond the confines of their situations: "One day I will say goodbye to Mango. I am too strong for her to keep me here forever. One day I will go away. Friends and neighbors will say, What happened to that Esperanza? Where did she go with all these books and paper? Why did she march so far away? They will not know I have gone away to come back. For the ones I left behind. For the ones who cannot out." In "Bums in the Attic," Esperanza says, "One day I'll own my own house, but I won't forget who or where I came from." The tension between Esperanza's emotional ties to this community and her desire to transcend it establish a sense of attraction and repulsion that characterize the work.

Kiki Cordero

Kiki, "with hair like fur," is Esperanza's younger brother.

Magdalena Cordero

"Nenny" is Esperanza's younger sister. Esperanza sees her little sister as childish and unable to understand the world as she does: "Nenny is too young to be my friend. She's just my sister and that was not my fault. You don't pick your sisters, you just get them and sometimes they come like Nenny." However, because the two girls have brothers, Esperanza understands that Nenny is her own responsibility to guide and protect. Esperanza and Nenny share common bonds both as sisters and as Chicana females. In the story "Laughter," a certain neighborhood house reminds both sisters of Mexico, a connection possible only because of their shared experience: "Nenny says: Yes, that's Mexico all right. That's what I was thinking exactly."

Mama Cordero

Esperanza's mother is typical of the women in Latin American communities whose life is defined by marriage, family, children, and traditionally female activities. Mama reveals herself as a superstitious figure who tells Esperanza that she was born on an evil day and that she will pray for her. Mama operates as a caretaker and has authority over her household, and she is portrayed as a martyr, sacrificing her own needs for those of her family. "I could've been somebody, you know?" Mama proclaims to Esperanza, explaining that she left school because she was ashamed that she didn't have nice clothes. Mama wishes for her daughters a better life outside the cycle of subjugation that characterizes her own, and she views education as the ticket out of that way of life.

Nenny Cordero

See Magdalena Cordero

Papa Cordero

Esperanza's father is portrayed as a man burdened with the obligation of providing for his family. Papa holds up a lottery ticket hopefully as he describes to the family the house they will buy one day. In the story "Papa Who Wakes Up Tired in the Dark," Papa reveals his vulnerability to Esperanza, his eldest child, when he learns of his own father's death and asks her to convey the news to her siblings while he returns to Mexico for the funeral.

Earl

This man with a southern accent, a jukebox repairman according to Esperanza, appears in the story "The Earl of Tennessee." He occupies a dark basement apartment and brings home women of ill repute whom Esperanza and her friends naively take to be his wife.

Elenita

Elenita, "witch woman" who tells fortunes with the help of Christian icons, tarot cards, and other accouterments, tells Esperanza after reading her cards that she sees a "home in the heart. This leaves Esperanza disappointed that a "real house" does not appear in her future.

Louie

The oldest in a family of girls, Louie and his family rent a basement apartment from Meme Ortiz' s mother. His cousin Marin lives with the family and helps take care of his younger sisters. Although

Louie is really her brother's friend, Esperanza notices that he "has two cousins and that his t-shirts never stay tucked in his pants."

Lucy

Lucy is a neighborhood girl whom Esperanza befriends even though her clothes "are crooked and old." Lucy and her sister Rachel are among the first friends Esperanza makes when she moves onto Mango Street.

Mamacita

In "No Speak English," Mamacita is the plump mother of a man across the street, a comic and tragic figure who stays indoors all the time because of her fear of speaking English.

Marin

Marin is a Puerto Rican neighbor, an older girl with whom Esperanza and her friends are fascinated. Marin wears makeup, sells Avon, and has a boyfriend in Puerto Rico whom she secretly intends to marry, but meanwhile, she is responsible for the care of her younger cousins.

Minerva

Minerva is a young woman not much older than Esperanza who "already has two kids and a husband who left."

Juan Ortiz

"Meme" is a neighbor of Esperanza's who has a large sheepdog. "The dog is big, like a man dressed in a dog suit, and runs the same way its owner does, clumsy and wild and with the limbs flopping all over the place like untied shoes."

Meme Ortiz

See Juan Ortiz

Rachel

Rachel is Lucy's sister, a sassy girl according to Esperanza. Esperanza and Lucy parade around the neighborhood in high heel shoes with her in the story "The Family of Little Feet."

Media Adaptations

- *The House on Mango Street* was adapted as a sound recording entitled *House on Mango Street; Woman Hollering Creek*, published by Random House in 1992. It is read by Sandra Cisneros.

Rafaela

Rafaela stays indoors and observes the world from her windowsill, "because her husband is afraid Rafaela will run away since she is too beautiful to look at." Rafaela stands as a symbol for the interior world of women on Mango Street, whose lives are circumscribed and bound by the structure of home and family.

Ruthie

Ruthie, "the only grown-up we know who likes to play," is a troubled, childlike woman whose husband left her and was forced to move from her own house in the suburbs back to Mango Street with her mother.

Sally

Sally wears black clothes, short skirts, nylons, and makeup. Esperanza looks upon her with fascination and wonder, and wants to emulate her, but the dark side of Sally's life is revealed in her relationship with her abusive father. She trades one type of ensnarement for another by marrying a marshmallow salesman before the eighth grade.

Sire

Sire is a young man who leers at Esperanza as she walks down the street, provoking in her inextricable feelings of desire, foreboding, and fear. Esperanza says that "it made your blood freeze to have somebody look at you like that."

The Three Sisters

"The Three Sisters" are Rachel and Lucy's elderly aunts who come to visit when Rachel and Lucy's baby sister dies. The three ladies recognize Esperanza's strong-willed nature, and plead with her not to forget the ones she leaves behind on Mango Street when she flees from there one day.

Rosa Vargas

In the story, "There Was an Old Woman She Had So Many Children She Didn't Know What to Do," Rosa is portrayed as a woman left in the lurch by a husband who abandoned her and their unruly kids. "They are bad those Vargas, and how can they help it with only one mother who is tired all the time from buttoning and bottling and babying, and who cries every day for the man who left without even leaving a dollar for bologna or a note explaining how come."

Themes

Coming of Age

Through various themes in *The House on Mango Street* Esperanza reveals herself as both a product of the community in which she lives and one of the only figures courageous enough to transcend her circumstances. Like all adolescents, Esperanza struggles to forge her own identity. In many respects, Esperanza's own keen observations and musings about the women in her neighborhood are her way of processing what will happen to her in the future and what is within her power to change. On the one hand, she is surrounded by adolescent myths and superstitions about sexuality. In the story "Hips," the adolescent Esperanza contemplates why women have hips: "The bones just one day open. One day you might decide to have kids, and then where are you going to put them?" Esperanza boldly experiments with the trappings of womanhood by wearing high heels in "The Family of Little Feet," and in "Sally," she looks enviously to the girl as an image of maturity: "My mother says to wear black so young is dangerous, but I want to buy shoes just like yours." However, Esperanza's brushes with sexuality are dangerous and negative in "The First Job" and "Red Clowns," and she feels betrayed by the way love is portrayed by her friends, the movies, and magazines. Esperanza observes characters such as Sally, Minerva, and Rafaela, who, through early and abusive marriages, are trapped in the neighborhood and into identifying themselves through their male connections. After witnessing this, Esperanza says in "Beautiful & Cruel," "I have decided not to grow up tame like the others who lay their necks on the threshold waiting for the ball and chain." Esperanza also forges her identity through the metaphor of the house. Her longing for a house of her own underscores her need for something uplifting and stable with which she can identify. Throughout the book there is a tension between Esperanza's ties to the *barrio* and her impressions of another kind of life outside of it. Ultimately, Esperanza's ability to see beyond her immediate surroundings allows her to transcend her circumstances and immaturity.

Culture and Heritage Difference

Esperanza keenly observes the struggles of Hispanic Americans who wish to preserve the essence of their heritage while striving to forge productive lives within American culture. It is through the sordid details of the lives of Esperanza's neighbors that we glimpse the humorous, moving, and tragic sides of these struggles. Esperanza's community serves as a microcosm of Latinos in America, and her own identity is interwoven with the identity of the neighborhood. People in the *barrio* relate to one another because of a shared past and current experience. In "Those Who Don't," Esperanza considers the stereotypes and fears that whites have of Latinos and vice versa. Cisneros weaves together popular beliefs, traditions, and other vestiges of the countries from which she and her neighbors trace their ancestry. In "No Speak English," for example, an old woman paints her walls pink to recall the colorful appearance of the houses in Mexico, a seemingly hopeless gesture in the drab underbelly of Chicago. She wails when her grandson sings the lyrics to an American television commercial but cannot speak Spanish. The tragic Mamacita risks losing her identity if she assimilates, like her little grandson, into American culture. In "Elenita, Cards, Palm, Water," the so-called "witch woman" of the neighborhood preserves the old wives' tales, superstitions, and traditional remedies for curing headaches, forgetting an old flame, and curing insomnia.

Despite these ties to the past, Esperanza leaves no doubt that she is destined to leave this neighborhood for a bigger world outside the *barrio*, an allusion to her dual cultural loyalties. Esperanza believes that one day she will own her own house outside the neighborhood. However, she also leaves no doubt that she will return one day for those unable to leave the environment on their own. In "Bums in the Attic," for example, she describes how she will let bums sleep in the attic of her house one day, "because I know how it is to be without a house." In "The Three Sisters," Esperanza gives further foreshadowing that she will one day leave Mango Street, but will return to help others. "You will always be Mango Street," three ladies tell her. "You can't erase what you know. You can't forget who you are." Esperanza leaves the reader with the notion that she will leave but will not forget her roots. Though she does not always want to belong to this environment, she realizes that her roots are too strong to resist. The books and papers Esperanza takes with her at the end of the book are her means of freedom from the ugly house and the social constraints on the neighborhood.

Gender Roles

The House on Mango Street is dedicated "a las Mujeres"—to the women. As the narrator, Esperanza offers the reader the greatest insights into the lives of female characters. One of the most enduring themes of the book is the socialization of females within Chicano society based on the fixed roles of the family. Cisneros explores the dynamics of women's lives within this precarious and male-dominated society, where the conditions of females are predetermined by economic and social constraints. For most women in the neighborhood, these constraints are too powerful to overcome. However, Esperanza possesses the power to see beyond her circumstances and the world of the ghetto, while those around her fall prey to it and perpetuate its cycle. Esperanza's mother is typical of a Hispanic woman grounded in this way of life.

Throughout the book, Esperanza deals with themes of womanhood, especially the role of single mothers. The interior world of females whose lives are tied to activities inside the house is contrasted with the external world of males, who go to work and operate in society at large. In "Boys & Girls," for example, Esperanza notes the difference between herself and her brothers: "The boys and the girls live in separate worlds. The boys in their universe and we in ours. My brothers for example. They've got plenty to say to me and Nenny inside the house. But outside they can't be seen talking to girls."

Topics for Further Study

- Characterize the social constraints of the women in Esperanza's neighborhood, and describe how Esperanza both responds to and transcends the social forces in her environment.

- Discuss the metaphor of the house in *The House on Mango Street*.

- Discuss *The House on Mango Street*

in relationship to the history of Mexican Americans in large cities of the United States.

Esperanza offers a feminine view of growing up in a Chicano neighborhood in the face of a socialization process that keeps women married, at home, and immobile within the society. The women in this book face domineering fathers and husbands, and raise children, often as single parents, under difficult circumstances. Many tales have tragic sides, such as those that paint the constrained existence of some of the women and girls in the neighborhood under the strong arm of husbands or fathers. The story "There Was an Old Woman She Had So Many Children She Didn't Know What to Do," tells of an abandoned young wife and her unruly children. In "Linoleum Roses," Sally is not allowed to talk on the phone or look out the window because of a jealous, domineering husband. Girls marry young in this society: "Minerva is only a little bit older than me but already she has two kids and a husband who left." But Esperanza is a courageous character who defies the stereotypes of Chicanas. She laments the attitudes that prevail in her community. Of her name, Esperanza says, "It was my great-grandmother's name and now it is mine. She was a horse woman too, born like me in the Chinese year of the horse— which is supposed to be bad luck if you're born female—but I think this is a Chinese lie because the Chinese, like the Mexicans, don't like their women strong." It is Esperanza's power to see beyond the barriers of her neighborhood, fueled by her education gained through reading and writing, that keep her from being trapped in the same roles as the women who surround her.

Point of View

The House on Mango Street is narrated by the adolescent Esperanza, who tells her story in the form of short, vivid tales. The stories are narrated in the first person ("I"), giving the reader an intimate glimpse of the girl's outlook on the world. Although critics often describe Esperanza as a childlike narrator, Cisneros said in a 1992 interview in *Interviews with Writers of the Post-Colonial World:* "If you take Mango Street and translate it, it's Spanish. The syntax, the sensibility, the diminutives, the way of looking at inanimate objects —that's not a child's voice as is sometimes said. That's Spanish! I didn't notice that when I was writing it." Incorporating and translating Spanish expressions literally into English, often without quotation marks, adds a singular narrative flavor that distinguishes Cisneros's work from that of her peers.

Setting

The House on Mango Street is set in a Latino neighborhood in Chicago. Esperanza briefly describes some of the rickety houses in her neighborhood, beginning with her own, which she says is "small and red with tight steps in front." Of Meme Ortiz's house, Esperanza says that "Inside the floors slant—And there are no closets. Out front there are twenty-one steps, all lopsided and jutting like crooked teeth." Mamacita's son paints the inside walls of her house pink, a reminder of the Mexican home she left to come to America. The furniture in Elena's house is covered in red fur and plastic. Esperanza gives the impression of a crowded neighborhood where people live in close quarters and lean out of windows, and where one can hear fighting, talking, and music coming from other houses on the street. Esperanza describes the types of shops in the concrete landscape of Mango Street: a laundromat, a junk store, the corner grocery. Cats, dogs, mice, and cockroaches make appearances at various times. However, while Esperanza gives fleeting glimpses of specific places, the images that the girl paints of her neighborhood are mostly understood through the people that inhabit it.

Structure

Just like Esperanza, whose identity isn't easy to define, critics have had difficulty classifying *The House on Mango Street.* Is it a collection of short stories? A novel? Essays? Autobiography? Poetry? Prose poems? The book is composed of very short, loosely organized vignettes. Each stands as a whole in and of itself, but collectively the stories cumulate in a mounting progression that creates an underlying coherence; the setting remains constant, and the same characters reappear throughout the tales. Cisneros once explained: "I wanted to write stories that were a cross between poetry and fiction—[I] wanted to write a collection which could be read at any random point without having any knowledge of what came before or after." Despite the disjunctive nature of the stories, as they evolve, Esperanza undergoes a maturation process, and she emerges at the end showing a more courageous and forthright facade.

Imagery

Despite certain underlying threads that link the tales in *The House on Mango Street*, the stories nonetheless remain disembodied from the kind of master narrative that typifies much of American fiction. The stories have a surreal and fragmented quality consistent with short, impressionistic glimpses into the mind of Esperanza. Rather than relying on long descriptive and narrative sequences that characterize many novels in English, Cisneros reveals dialogue and evokes powerful imagery with few words. With a minimum number of words, Cisneros includes humorous elements like the nicknames of her playmates, family, and neighbors —Nenny, Meme, and Kiki, for example. But she also, with few descriptive elements, evokes the ugliness of violence and sexual aggression swirling around her in the *barrio*. The author's carefully crafted, compact sentences convey poignant meanings that can be read on different levels. Seemingly simple dialogue reveals deeper, underlying concerns of the narrator. A straightforward dialogue between Esperanza and Nenny about a house that reminded the girls of

Mexico in the story "Laughter," for example, evokes the connection of the girls to one another and to the country of their heritage. The bizarre yet moving experiences of Esperanza evoke a social commentary but do not explicitly state it. Cisneros strikes a tenuous balance between humor and pathos, between tragic and comic elements.

Symbols

Several important symbolic elements characterize *The House on Mango Street*. First, the image of the house is a powerful one. The house that Esperanza lives in—small, crooked, drab—contrasts with the image of the house that Esperanza imagines for herself in "Bums in the Attic": "I want a house on a hill like the ones with the gardens where Papa works." But the metaphor of the house is more than pure materialism. The house represents everything that Esperanza does not have—financial means and pleasant surroundings—but more importantly, it represents stability, triumph, and transcendence over the pressures of the neighborhood. Throughout the book, especially in stories such as "The House on Mango Street," and "A Rice Sandwich," Esperanza struggles with the embarrassment of poverty: "You live *there?* The way she [aunt] said it made me feel like nothing. *There. I lived there."* Another important symbol in the book are the trappings of womanhood—shoes, makeup, black clothes—that fascinate and intimidate the adolescent Esperanza, who carefully observes the other women in her community.

Although at times these signs of womanhood leave Esperanza feeling betrayed, in "Beautiful & Cruel," she sees them as potential for power: "In the movies there is always one with red red lips who is beautiful and cruel. She is the one who drives the men crazy and laughs them all away. Her power is her own. She will not give it away."

Tone

Cisneros's writing is often compared to music for its poetic, lyrical quality. *The House on Mango Street* has a strong aural character, and the author clearly has an interest in sound that comes through in much of her poetry. Esperanza speaks in a singsong voice, with the repetitive quality of a nursery rhyme. Cisneros's tone is at once youthful and lighthearted, but displays a tragic or menacing tone at times. Cisneros once commented, "I wanted stories like poems, compact and lyrical and ending with reverberation." In her more recent works, Cisneros has outgrown the girlish voice of Esperanza and takes on more mature themes while retaining this distinctive lyrical quality in her writing.

Mexican Immigration to the United States

Cisneros plays on her dual Mexican American heritage throughout her work, and *The House on Mango Street* in particular reflects the experience of Mexicans in the United States. In the midnineteenth century, Mexico ceded its northern territories (present-day California, Arizona, and New Mexico) to the United States at the end of the Mexican War, and Mexican landowners lost many of their rights under the Treaty of Guadalupe Hidalgo. From about 1900 to 1920, immigrants from Mexico were actively recruited into the United States as low-cost labor for railroad, mining, and other industries, especially throughout the southwestern United States. Mexican immigration was widespread and unregulated through the 1920s, when immigration from Mexico and some other countries hit its peak. Between World War I and World War II, however, Mexican immigration came to a halt due in part to the pressures of the Great Depression, and Mexican Americans faced repatriation, poverty, and rampant discrimination.

Despite their contribution and service to the U.S. Army during World War II, Mexican Americans continued to face discrimination upon returning home after World War II. For example, many Mexican Americans were treated like second-class citizens. And throughout the fifties and sixties, despite their eagerness to integrate more fully into American society, Mexican Americans were still treated as "outsiders" by mainstream American culture. Despite their push for civil rights throughout the 1960s and the 1970s, many Chicanos still faced discrimination that limited opportunities for advancement. By 1983, when *The House on Mango Street* was published, stringent U.S. immigration laws had long limited the number of Mexicans who were allowed to immigrate to the United States. Those who had immigrated legally or been born in America still experienced stereotyping and biases in American culture at large. In "Those Who Don't," Cisneros evokes the stereotyping of Mexican Americans: "Those who don't know any better come into our neighborhood scared. They think we're dangerous. They think we will attack them with shiny knives."

Because of the discrimination often leveled at Spanish-speaking populations by English-speaking Americans, many Mexican Americans choose to resist speaking Spanish except among family within the privacy of their homes. Cisneros, for example, remembers that she only spoke Spanish with her father at home, while otherwise being fully integrated within the mainstream American educational system. On the other hand, other Mexican Americans, particularly those of the older generations who retained a nostalgia for their mother country, never relinquished the use of Spanish as their primary tongue. In *The House on*

Mango Street, for example, Mamacita consciously refused to speak English because for her it represented a blatant rejection of her past and her identity, and she limited her English vocabulary to "He not here," "No speak English," and "Holy smokes." Esperanza's father remembers eating nothing but "hamandeggs" when he first arrived in the United States because it was the only English phrase he knew. In the United States today, there is a renewed interest among the younger generation of Mexican Americans to learn and more fully appreciate the Spanish language.

Hispanic American Population and Culture

The largest number of Mexican Americans in the United States are concentrated in southern California and Texas, with another sizable population in New York City. As one of the largest cities in the United States, Chicago historically has also attracted immigrants from around the world, including those from Mexico. Cisneros and her mother were born in the United States, as are many of the characters in *The House on Mango Street*. Nevertheless, they retain strong ties with their Mexican heritage and are integrated into the Mexican American communities throughout the country. In different parts of the country, these groups are referred to as "Mexican American," "Mexicanos," "Chicanos," and sometimes by the more general terms "Hispanics" or "Latinos," which collectively describes people from those cultures colonized by Spain from the fifteenth century to the present, including Cuba, Puerto Rico, Mexico, and many other countries. The population of Hispanics in the United States continues to swell, and by some estimates, they will make up about thirteen percent of the nation's population by the early years of the twenty-first century.

Historically, Mexican American men and women have suffered negative stereotyping and prejudices that prevented them from securing desirable jobs and being upwardly mobile within the society. Therefore, many remain concentrated in low-income neighborhoods like the one portrayed in *The House on Mango Street*. Poverty is a reality faced by many Mexican American populations living in the United States. In *The House on Mango Street*, the theme of poverty pervades the stories. In "Alicia Who Sees Mice," for example, the mice are a symbol of poverty. Alicia, who stays up late studying because she "doesn't want to spend her whole life in a factory or behind a rolling pin," sees the mice scurrying around after dark, a symbol of her circumstances in the neighborhood. In *The House on Mango Street*, the source of Esperanza's embarrassment about her house and her circumstances derives from the poverty that many Mexican Americans face. In "Bums in the Attic," the economic disparity between "people who live on hills" and those who live in the *barrio* is clear.

The role of women within the history of the Hispanic community is significant. Although in *The*

House on Mango Street and other works by Cisneros, some Mexican American women are portrayed as trapped within a cycle of socialization, Cisneros noted in a 1992 interview in *Interviews with Writers of the Post-Colonial World*, "I have to say that the traditional role is kind of a myth. The traditional Mexican woman is a fierce woman. There's a lot of victimization but we are also fierce. We are very fierce."

Cisneros says she was influenced by American and British writers throughout high school, and she remembers reading works such as Lewis Carroll's *Alice's Adventures in Wonderland.* But only when she was introduced to the Chicago writing scene in college and graduate school did Cisneros come in contact with Chicano writers. Later, Chicano writers like Gary Soto, Loma Dee Cervantes, and Alberto Ríos were also among her circle of colleagues. Today, Sandra Cisneros stands foremost among Chicana writers who emerged in the 1980s, including Ana Castillo, Denise Chávez, and Gloria Anzaldúa.

Critical Overview

Although *The House on Mango Street* is Cisneros's first novel and appeared without high expectations, over time it has become well known and lauded by critics. Bebe Moore Campbell, writing in *New York Times Book Review*, called *The House on Mango Street* a "radiant first collection." The book, published in 1983, has provided Cisneros broad exposure as a writer. Her works are not numerous, but this book established the author as a major figure in contemporary American literature. Her work has already been the subject of scholarly works by historians of Chicana and women's studies. In 1985, it was awarded the Before Columbus American Book Award. Today many high schools and university departments, including Women's Studies, Ethnic Studies, English, and Creative Writing, use the book in college courses. Cisneros has read her poetry at several conferences and has won several grants and awards in the United States and abroad.

Critics usually discuss the importance of *The House on Mango Street* in terms of its incisive portrayal of the race-class-gender paradigm that characterizes the Hispanic experience in the United States. The book eloquently expresses the tensions of growing up a minority in a white-dominated society and growing up a woman in a male-dominated society, accompanied by feelings of alienation and loneliness, change and transformation. Like many Chicano writers, Cisneros touches on themes of overcoming the burden of race, gender, and class, with which all the women in the book are strapped to a greater or lesser extent. Her vivid and powerful descriptions combined with her funny and compelling dialogue persuasively capture the essence of women's lives within this precarious society.

Critics also comment on the particularly feminine viewpoint of the socialization process that Cisneros offers as an important element of the work. In this regard, Cisneros parallels the work of other Chicana writers, forging a viewpoint heretofore only offered by male Hispanic American authors. Cisneros notes that it has taken longer for female Chicana writers to get educated and make contributions parallel to those of the male Chicano writers who have been publishing works a few decades longer. Esperanza is portrayed as a bold girl who experiments with nontraditional roles of females within her society: "I have begun my own kind of war. Simple. Sure. I am one who leaves the table like a man, without putting back the chair or picking up the plate." Cisneros says that she writes about the things that haunt her from her past. "In my writing as well as in that of other Chicanas and other women, there is the necessary phase of dealing with those ghosts and voices most urgently haunting us, day by day."

Throughout her education Cisneros was exposed to mainstream English writing, and thus she began her own writing by imitating these authors. Her first poems were published in the journals *Nuestro* and *Revista Chicano-Riqueña*, which gave Cisneros the confidence to turn to major book publishers thereafter. Although *The House on Mango Street* took five years to complete, she found her own voice and her own literary direction. Most critics comment on Cisneros's ability to convey powerful images through short, compact statements, and to vividly portray an experience or feeling in just a few words. Eduardo F. Elias noted that, "Hers is the work of a poet, a painter with words, who relies on sounds, plural meanings, and resonances to produce rich and varied images in each reader's mind."

Cisneros has won numerous prestigious awards, most notably the 1985 Before Columbus American Book Award, and has read her poetry in public both in the United States and abroad. In the late 1980s, Cisneros spent time in Austin, Texas under a Paisano Dobie Fellowship, and won first and third prizes in the Segundo Concurso Nacional del Cuento Chicano from the University of Arizona for some of her short stories. In 1992 she received a National Endowment for the Arts grant, which permitted her to travel in Europe and develop new themes for her work. In the spring of 1993 she was in residence at the Fondation Michael Karolyi in Vence, France. Prior to winning these awards, she taught at Latino Youth Alternative High School in Chicago from 1978 to 1980. Her work is widely studied in the university and high school settings, and it fits well into different disciplines, including Women's Studies, American literature, and Mexican

American history.

Sources

Bebe Moore Campbell, "Crossing Borders," *New York Times Book Review*, May 26, 1991, p. 6.

Sandra Cisneros, "Interview with Sandra Cisneros," in Reed Dasenbrock and Feroza Jussawalla, *Interviews with Writers of the Post-Colonial World*, University Press of Mississippi, 1992.

Eduardo F. Elias, "Sandra Cisneros," *Dictionary of Literary Biography, Volume 122: Chicano Writers, Second Series* edited by Francisco A. Lomeli and Carl Shirley, Gale Research, 1992, pp. 77-81.

Eduardo F. Elias, "The House on Mango Street," *Reference Guide to American Literature*, 3rd edition, edited by Jim Kamp, Gale Research, 1994, p. 992.

Eduardo F. Elias, "Sandra Cisneros," *Reference Guide to American Literature*, 3rd edition, edited by Jim Kamp, Gale Research, 1994, pp. 200-02.

For Further Study

Pilar E. Rodriguez Aranda, interview in *The Americas Review*, Spring, 1990, pp. 64-80.

> An interview with Cisneros which focuses on the writing of *The House on Mango Street* as well as on the general trend of Latinas "reinventing themselves" in relation to their culture.

Maria Elena de Valdes, "In Search of Identity in Cisneros's *The House on Mango Street,*" in *The Canadian Review of American Studies*, Volume 23:1 (Fall), 1992, pp. 55-72.

> Emphasizes the importance of Esperanza's "highly lyrical" narrative voice.

Erlinda Gonzalez-Berry and Tey Diana Rebolledo, "Growing Up Chicano: Tomas Rivera and Sandra Cisneros," in *Revista Chicano-Riquena*, Volume 13:34, 1985, pp. 109-19.

> Considers Cisneros' novel as an example of the growing up story which forms a general theme in Chicano literature.

Ellen McCracken, "Sandra Cisneros' The *House on Mango Street:* Community-Oriented Introspection and the Demystification of Patriarchal Violence," in *Breaking Boundaries: Latina Writing and Critical*

Readings, edited by Anuncion Horno-Delgado, Eliana Ortega, Nina M. Scott, Nancy Saporta Steinbach, University of Massachusetts Press, 1989, pp. 62-71.

> Discusses *The House on Mango Street* as a "marginalized text" which contradicts the individualistic values of the male-dominated literary canon.

Julián Olivares, "Sandra Cisneros' The House on Mango Street, and the Poetics of Space," in *Chicana Creativity and Criticism: Charting New Frontiers in American Literature*, Arte Público, 1988, pp. 160-69.

> Claims that Cisneros "employs her imagery as a poetics of space," but reverses the conventional emphasis on the home as a site of comfort and the outside world as a source of anxiety.

Renato Rosaldo, "Fables of the Fallen Guy," in *Criticism in the Borderlands: Studies in Chicano Literature, Culture and Ideology*, edited by Hector Calderon and Jose David Saldivar, Duke University Press, 1991, pp. 84-93.

> Situates *The House on Mango Street* and Cisneros in the context of earlier narratives of cultural authenticity written by Latino writers featuring male warrior-heroes.

Ramón Saldívar, "The Dialectics of Subjectivity: Gender and Difference in Isabella Rios, Sandra Cisneros, and Cherrie Moraga," in *Chicano Narrative: The Dialectics of Difference*, University of Wisconsin Press, 1990, pp. 171-99.

> Discusses the intersection of race, gender, and class in *The House on Mango Street.*